A Note to Parents

Dorling Kindersley *Readers* is a compelling new program for beginning readers, designed in conjunction with leading literacy experts, including Dr. Linda Gambrell, President of the National Reading Conference and past board member of the International Reading Association.

Beautiful illustrations and superb full-color photographs combine with engaging, easy-to-read stories to offer a fresh approach to each subject in the series. Each Dorling Kindersley *Reader* is guaranteed to capture a child's interest while developing his or her reading skills, general knowledge, and love of reading.

The four levels of Dorling Kindersley *Readers* are aimed at different reading abilities, enabling you to choose the books that are exactly right for your child:

Level 1 for **Preschool to Grade 1**
Level 2 for **Grades 1 to 3**
Level 3 for **Grades 2 and 3**
Level 4 for **Grades 2 to 4**

The "normal" age at which a child begins to read can be anywhere from three to eight years old, so these levels are intended only as a general guideline.

No matter which level you select, you can be sure that you are helping your child learn to read, then read to learn!

Dorling  Kindersley

LONDON, NEW YORK, SYDNEY, DELHI, PARIS,
MUNICH and JOHANNESBURG

Produced by NFL Publishing Group
Vice-President/Editor in Chief
John Wiebusch
Managing Editor Chuck Garrity, Sr.
Project Editor James Buckley, Jr.
Art Director Bill Madrid

For DK Publishing
Editor Regina Kahney
Reading Consultant
Linda Gambrell, Ph.D.

First American Edition, 2000
Published in the United States by
Dorling Kindersley, Inc.
95 Madison Ave., New York, NY 10016

2 4 6 8 10 9 7 5 3 1

Library of Congress Catalog #00-024795

ISBN 0-7894-6379-2 (hc)
ISBN 0-7894-6756-9 (pb)

Printed in China

All Photographs are Copyright © NFL Photos.
t=top, b=below, l=left, r=right,
c=center, FC=front cover
AquaViva: 22bl; **Vernon Biever:** 8tl, 9tr, 12bl; **Scott
Cunningham:** 28tl, 34tl; **David Drapkin:** 37tr, 38b, 38tr, 41br;
Malcolm Emmons: 13tr; **Thearon Henderson:** 32b; **Allen
Kee:** 42t, 44b; **NFL Photos:** 4tl, 4bl, 5r, 16bl, 17tr, 18tr, 19tr,
19br, 20tl, 21br; **Daryl Norenberg:** FCr, 10tl; **Pro Football
Hall of Fame:** 16tl, 18bl; **Richard Raphael:** 6bl, 24tl, 24br,
25tr; **Kevin Reece:** 15br; **Joe Robbins:** 40tl, 41tr; **Manny
Rubio:** 36b; **James D. Smith:** 42b; 43t, 45t, 45b; **Jay Spencer:**
11r; **Paul Spinelli/NFL Photos:** 34b; **RH Stagg:** 18bl; **David
Stluka:** 29b; **Kevin Terrell/NFL Photos:** 31bl, 31tr, 33tr;
Tony Tomsic: 7tr, 15tr, 20bl, 23tr, 40br; **Greg Trott:** FCbl,
30bl, 30br, 33br; **Shawn Wood:** 10bl, 18tl.
Illust.: **Merv Corning:** 9br; **Roger Motzkus** 14bl, 26bl.

see our complete
catalog at
www.dk.com

Contents

NFL'S GREATEST UPSETS

Written by James Buckley, Jr.

DK
A Dorling Kindersley Book

"Any given Sunday"

The National Football League has been around since 1920. One of its oldest sayings (even though no one is sure who said it first) is that "on any given Sunday, any team in the league can be a winner."

Of course, some teams are better than others. One team might enter the game with a better record, with better players, or more all-stars. One team might be "favored" to win; in other words, most people think that team will win.

But in the NFL, that doesn't matter. You can't win a game on your reputation. You can't win a game because people think you will. You have to win on the field.

When a lesser team defeats a better team, the result is called an "upset." This is different than an upset stomach, though the losing team has plenty of that afterward.

Leather helmets
Players in the early days of the NFL wore flimsy leather helmets like this one.

For the legs
Early football pants were made from leather and canvas.

A victory by an underdog—that's another name for the team that wasn't supposed to win—can be very memorable for the team and its fans.

Many of the most memorable games in NFL history were upsets. This book presents a look at some of the greatest upsets in NFL history.

Winner! Jets coach Weeb Ewbank, quarterback Joe Namath, and Namath's father John in the Jets' locker room after Super Bowl III.

The old AFL
The American Football League was founded in 1960 with eight teams.

"I guarantee it"

From 1960 to 1969, the American Football League (AFL) was a rival to the older National Football League (NFL). Although the AFL had top-notch players, NFL fans felt that the AFL was an inferior league. NFL players called the AFL the "Mickey Mouse League." But AFL players knew they could compete with the "big boys."

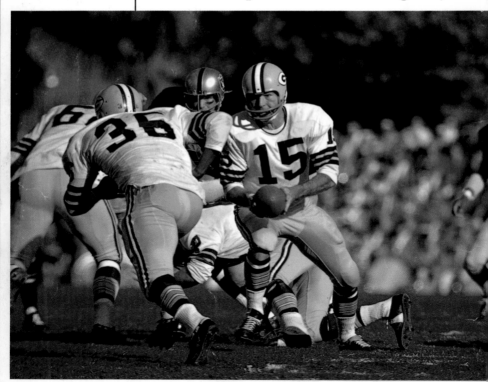

Quarterback Bart Starr (15) was the MVP of Green Bay's two Super Bowl triumphs.

Beginning in 1967, the champions of the AFL and the NFL met in a postseason championship game that would become known as the Super Bowl. The Green Bay Packers of the NFL won Super Bowls I and II, defeating the AFL's Kansas City Chiefs and Oakland Raiders.

The Packers' victories added to the feeling most people had—that the NFL was better than the AFL.

In 1968, the New York Jets won the AFL championship and a berth in Super Bowl III. Most people thought they would suffer the same fate as Kansas City and Oakland. Although the AFL, and the Jets, had some good players, no one thought they could hold up against the NFL's best.

The Jets faced the Baltimore Colts of the NFL, one of the most powerful teams in recent years.

Lombardi
Coach Vince Lombardi led Green Bay to five NFL championships in the 1960s.

TM/©1968 NFL

Big game
The third Super Bowl was held in the Orange Bowl stadium in Miami, Florida.

Astronauts
Three Apollo 8 astronauts—James Lovell, Frank Borman, and William Anders—led the fans at Super Bowl III in the Pledge of Allegiance.

Trademark
Namath was one of the first players to wear white football cleats.

The Colts boasted a strong defense, led by Mike Curtis and Bubba Smith. On offense, they were led by quarterback Earl Morrall, who had been the NFL's most valuable player that season. In reserve, they had Johnny Unitas, one of the greatest quarterbacks in NFL history. However, Unitas was near the end of his brilliant career, was injured, and would not start in the Super Bowl.

Baltimore had won several championships in previous years, and nearly everyone expected them to win again. They had posted a 15-1 record that season, including two playoff victories.

The Jets were led by a wily veteran coach named Weeb Ewbank, powerful runner Matt Snell, and Joe Namath, a quarterback with a rocket arm and a big smile.

If anyone could show the NFL that the AFL was just as good, it was Namath. In his third season out of the University of Alabama, Namath was as well known for his confident attitude as he was for the amazingly quick release of his passes.

Early in the week before the game, he said something that would make him more famous than anything he had done on the field. He made a statement that would live forever in NFL history.

When asked if the Jets would win the game, he said, "I guarantee it."

Namath was as well-known for his wild personal style as for his accurate arm and quick release.

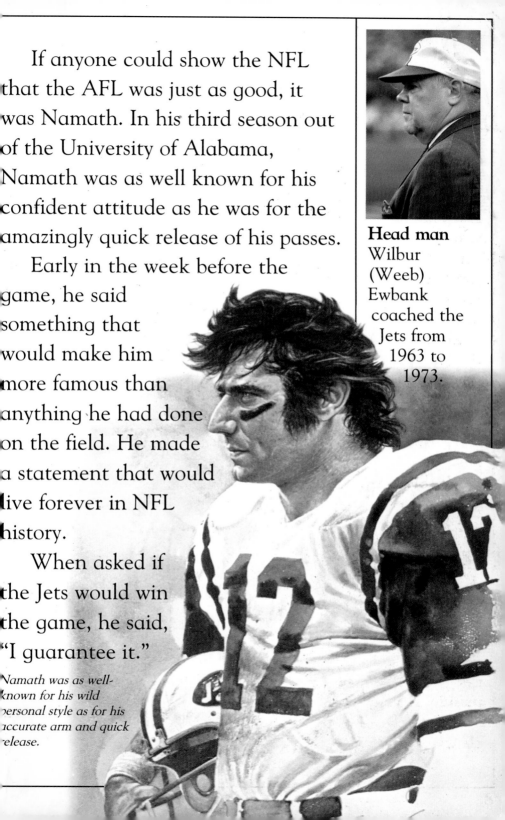

Head man Wilbur (Weeb) Ewbank coached the Jets from 1963 to 1973.

King Colt
Don Shula coached the Colts in Super Bowl III. He later became the NFL's all-time winningest coach.

Kicking shoe
In the 1960s, kickers used special shoes with square toes like this one.

That was the sort of thing that football players just did not do. To "guarantee" a victory pumped up opponents to make sure it didn't come true.

But Namath had said it. It was done. Now it was up to him and his teammates to make it stand up.

At game time, fans were predicting that Baltimore would win by more than 18 points. Colts' owner Carroll Rosenbloom had hired a band for his postgame "victory" party.

Just one thing: First, they had to play the game.

Shortly after the opening kickoff, the Colts looked like a team that was trying to lose, not win.

A receiver dropped a pass in the end zone; if he had caught it there, it would have been a touchdown.

In the first half, Colts kicker Lou Michaels missed a short field goal. Morrall threw an interception. That pattern of mistakes would be repeated by Baltimore all game long.

Overall, the Colts threw four interceptions, lost one fumble, missed two field-goal attempts, and had a wide-open receiver in the end zone, but didn't throw to him.

In Super Bowl III, Namath completed 17 of 28 passes for 206 yards.

Power runner Running back Matt Snell scored the Jets' only touchdown in Super Bowl III on a 4-yard run. He ran for 121 yards in the game.

Namath took advantage of Baltimore's mistakes. Following a Jets' interception of a pass by Morrall, Namath led New York on an 80-yard drive that ended with a 4-yard touchdown run by Snell.

To the surprise of everyone except the Jets, New York led the mighty Colts 7-0 at halftime.

Another Colts fumble led to a field goal by the Jets' Jim Turner early in the second half.

Turner made a second field goal soon after that made the score 13-0. The Colts could not believe it. How could an AFL team be leading them in the Super Bowl?

Late in the third quarter, Colts coach Don Shula turned to his bench and motioned for Unitas.

"All of a sudden, I was scared to death," said Ewbank, who had coached the Colts from 1954 to 1962. "We had seen him make so many big plays for so long."

Old high tops Colts quarterback Johnny Unitas was well-known for his high-topped black shoes. He was also one of the greatest ever to play his position.

But Unitas was not enough. He led the Colts to a touchdown, but it was too little, too late.

Incredibly, the underdog Jets had defeated the powerful Colts 16-7 in the greatest upset in Super Bowl history.

Merger
A merger
occurs when
two companies,
or in this case
leagues,
become one.

The game affected pro football beyond the score and the record book. The following year, the NFL and the AFL completed their long-planned merger.

But instead of joining the NFL as second-class citizens, the Jets and the other AFL teams came in as respected clubs. The Jets had showed that the AFL was good enough to compete in the NFL.

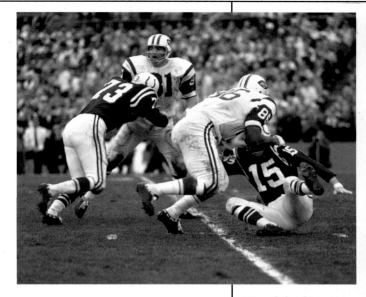

For his part, Namath's legend was secure. He had "guaranteed" an impossible victory, then made his words come true.

No one in the crowd believed they could do it, but the Jets did.

"Joe really believed what he said before the game," Jets tackle Dave Herman said. "He really thought we were going to beat them. Eventually, we all believed it."

The lasting image from the game is of Namath running off the field, waving his index finger in the air to show just who was Number One.

Tackled! Jets defenders made life miserable for Earl Morrall.

In the Hall Namath was elected to the Pro Football Hall of Fame in 1985.

"They don't like us"

Another small league had joined the NFL in 1950. Three teams from the All-America Football Conference (AAFC) became part of the larger NFL. One was the Cleveland Browns, who had won all four AAFC championships.

NFL champs
This is a program from the 1949 NFL Championship Game won by the Eagles.

In another league
The AAFC played from 1946 to 1949. In 1950, the Browns, the San Francisco 49ers, and the Baltimore Colts joined the NFL.

The Browns used the passing game more effectively than any other team. Their leader was quarterback Otto Graham (left), who would become one of the most successful quarterbacks in NFL history.

PAUL BROWN

The Browns' coach was Paul Brown, and he was regarded as an offensive wizard. He created many new plays and formations. Brown is credited with revolutionizing the way that coaches do their jobs.

But for all their talent and success, the Browns were coming from what many considered to be a second-class league. For their first game in the NFL, the older league gave the Browns a huge challenge: the Philadelphia Eagles.

The Eagles had been the NFL champions in 1948 and 1949, and were favored over the upstarts from the "other league."

In the cards
Coach Paul Brown led the Cleveland Browns to seven championships in 10 years from 1946 to 1955.

Two for two
The Eagles won both the 1948 and 1949 NFL titles by shutting out their opponents, a feat still unmatched.

Philadelphia had become a great team by stopping i opponents from gaining ground by running the ball.

But they had never seen anythin like the Browns' passing attack, whic Graham ran to perfection.

Eagles coach Earle (Greasy) Neal said that Paul Brown should coach basketball instead of football "because he puts the ball in the air so often!"

Brown was confident, however.

"There isn't a defensive back live who can keep up with our eceivers," he said.

Brown also used the NFL's pinion of the AAFC to inspire is players.

"We're new and they don't like s," Brown said before the game.

The game began as most fans redicted, with the Eagles grabbing n early 3-0 lead.

But the second time the Browns ad the ball, Graham teamed with receiver Dub Jones on a 59-yard touchdown play. Soon after, Graham passed 26 yards to Dante Lavelli for another touchdown.

To everyone's surprise, the Browns led at halftime, 14-3.

Wide receiver Mac Speedie hauls in a pass from Graham. Note the leather helmets of the time...without facemasks.

Thoughtful
Brown almost always wore a gray or brown hat while coaching.

First strike
In 1951, Cleveland's Dub Jones set an NFL record by scoring 6 touchdowns in one game.

In the third quarter, one of the Browns' greatest players put on a defensive show.

Today's NFL players play only offense or defense. In 1950, many players played on both sides of the ball. For Cleveland, Marion Motley was a powerful, bruising running back, but he was also a great linebacker.

In the third quarter, he made four key tackles to keep Philadelphia from scoring from the 6-yard line.

By the end of the game, the Browns were running and passing at will. The final score was Cleveland 35, Philadelphia 10.

The Browns had arrived in the NFL with a bang. Called a "minor-league" team before the game, they proved they belonged.

Special ball
Many NFL teams celebrate important victories by having a football specially painted.

Next job
In 1968, Paul Brown became the founder and first coach of another NFL team, the Cincinnati Bengals.

In fact, they belonged at the top. In 1950, Cleveland won the league championship, defeating the Rams 30-28. Graham would lead the team to five more NFL Championship Games and two more NFL titles.

And it all started with a big upset.

Cheers! After winning the 1950 NFL championship, the Browns celebrated in the team locker room. Coach Brown, with hat on, is at the center.

NFL stars
The Dallas Cowboys joined the NFL in 1960. Their "star" logo comes from the nickname of their state, Texas: the Lone Star State.

"A very lucky play"

From 1971 to 1973, the Dallas Cowboys were in three NFC Championship Games. In 1974, they dropped to an 8-6 record. In 1975, they finished 10-4, but some people thought they were lucky to have done that well.

By that season, several key veterans had retired, and the team had a dozen rookies on the roster. That is why they were big underdogs entering their 1975 playoff game at Minnesota against the Vikings.

The Vikings' "Purp People Eaters" wer legendar

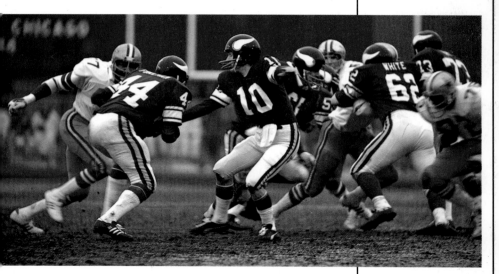

The Vikings were the best team in the NFC in 1975. They were even more dominant than their 12-2 record showed. They had allowed the fewest yards in the NFC. Their front defensive four were known as the "Purple People Eaters." Quarterback Fran Tarkenton was among the game's best.

On a cold, gray day in Minnesota, the teams met in the NFC Divisional Playoff Game.

To win, the Cowboys sent up a prayer to the football gods that is still spoken of today.

Fran the man
Quarterback Fran Tarkenton (10) led the Vikings to three Super Bowls.

Up north
The Vikings joined the NFL in 1961. The horns on their helmets echo Viking symbols.

Chief Cowboy
While at the Naval Academy, Roger Staubach won the 1963 Heisman Trophy as the nation's top college football player.

The first quarter was scoreless. Minnesota scored in the second quarter on a 1-yard run by Chuck Foreman.

Quarterback Roger Staubach led the Cowboys on a 72-yard drive that ended with a 4-yard touchdown run by Doug Dennison.

A field goal by Dallas's Toni Fritsch gave the Cowboys the lead early in the fourth quarter.

But Tarkenton was not through. He had made his reputation on his ability to run with the ball, to "scramble" out of trouble. Tarkenton ran or passed for 57 of Minnesota's 70 yards on a long drive in the fourth quarter.

McClanahan scored to put the Vikings ahead in the fourth quarter.

At the end of the drive, Brent McClanahan scored on a 1-yard plunge.

After a Cowboys' punt, the Dallas defense stopped the Vikings. Staubach and the Cowboys were deep in their own territory with less than two minutes remaining. Things did not look good.

They didn't get much better. Three plays later, the Cowboys faced fourth-and-16.

"Got any ideas?" Staubach asked in the huddle.

"I think I can beat my man on a corner pattern to the right," wide receiver Drew Pearson said.

"Okay, let's try it," Staubach replied.

Huddle up!
Before most plays, football teams gather in a "huddle" around the quarterback to learn what play the team will run.

25

Pass defense
Defenders called safeties and cornerbacks try to stop receivers from catching the ball.

Surprise score
Drew Pearson (88) cradles the ball on his hip and tiptoes into the end zone for the winning score.

The football, Pearson, and Vikings cornerback Nate Wright all met at the 50-yard line. If Pearson were to miss, the game would be over moments later.

He made the catch...Dallas had another chance!

Pearson was gasping for air when he went back to the huddle. Dallas ran one play while he caught his breath.

"I'm ready now," Pearson said.

What happened next was one of the most famous—and unexpected—plays in NFL history.

From the 50-yard line, Pearson took off down the right sideline. Staubach took the snap and launched a high, arcing pass toward the end zone.

It came up just a bit short.

Pearson and the Vikings' Wright saw the ball in the air and both slowed down. Then Wright fell.

The ball hit Pearson on the hip, and he smothered it with one hand. Still running, he held it tightly against his hip and stepped into the end zone. Touchdown, Dallas! And with it came one surprising upset.

"It was just a 'Hail Mary' pass," Staubach said afterward of the "prayer" he sent up. "A very, very lucky play."

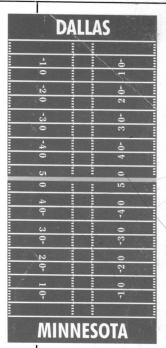

Midfield
The midfield line (here in yellow) of the 100-yard football field is called the 50-yard line.

"A very special day"

In 1995, the NFL added two new teams. The Carolina Panthers and the Jacksonville Jaguars were called expansion teams because the league "expanded" when they joined.

No one expects an expansion team to be good in its first season. Many of the players are young and inexperienced. Some are old and near the end of their careers. The team also has not played together for very long. Before 1995, no team in NFL history had won even four games in its first season.

But in Carolina's first NFL season, the Panthers proved many of those things false.

Their season started as many expected. The Panthers lost their first five games. But the team learned during those losses, and they improved every week.

Eye black
Players, such as Carolina's Kerry Collins, often wear black grease high on their cheeks to reduce glare.

What's a panther?
A large (100-150 pounds), usually black member of the cat family that lives in Asia and Africa.

Their first victory of the season came against the New York Jets.

The Panthers followed that with wins over the New Orleans Saints and the New England Patriots.

But their next opponent would be the new team's biggest challenge yet: a game played against the 49ers in San Francisco.

What's a jaguar?
A spotted member of the large cat family that lives in South America.

The first NFL game for Jacksonville and Carolina came against each other in August, 1995.

The 49ers were the defending NFL champions. The previous January, they had won Super Bowl XXIX. An expansion team had never defeated a defending Super Bowl champion.

Would the Carolina Panthers be the first?

Right away, things were looking up for the Panthers. Carolina linebacker Sam Mills forced a fumble by San Francisco's Brent Jones.

Why 49ers? In 1849, gold was discovered in northern California. Thousands of people rushed to the San Francisco area and were called "49ers."

After intercepting Grbac's pass, McKyer headed toward the end zone.

The Panthers recovered the fumble. A few plays later, John Kasay kicked a 39-yard field goal that gave the Panthers a 3-0 lead.

The mighty 49ers marched right back down the field.

San Francisco quarterback Elvis Grbac [GUR-bak] dropped back to pass. He threw toward the end zone, but his pass was intercepted.

Carolina's Tim McKyer grabbed the pass and raced 96 yards for a touchdown.

"I saw Tim grab the ball and I thought, 'Oh, baby! Home sweet home,'" Mills said after the game. "That was a very big play."

The "foot" in football
Kickers make a field goal and earn three points for their team by kicking the ball from the ground over the crossbar and between the uprights of the goalposts.

All-time great
Jerry Rice is the NFL's all-time leader in receptions, receiving yards, and touchdowns.

Fumble forcer
Panthers cornerback Tyrone Poole (below) made a big play by knocking the ball out of Taylor's hands.

Leading 10-0, the Panthers again turned to their defense for a big play. Early in the second quarter, Jerry Rice, the 49ers' star receiver, caught a pass and headed for the end zone.

But Carolina's Tyrone Poole chased Rice. He reached out and punched the ball out of Rice's hands. It was another fumble!

The ball went through the end zone for a "touchback," which gave Carolina the ball.

Panthers quarterback Kerry Collins led his team on a march that ended with a 47-yard field goal by Kasay.

At halftime, the score was Carolina 13, San Francisco 0. The 49ers' fans booed as their heroes ran off the field. The fans couldn't believe their eyes!

In the second half, things didn't get much better for the home team. The Panthers forced a fumble by John Taylor, another top receiver.

Poole, a rookie, again did the honors, knocking the ball out of Taylor's hands near the goal line.

The young "kids" on the Panthers were showing the veterans a few new tricks.

But would their lead hold up against the defending Super Bowl champions?

Tough job
Pass defenders must watch the receiver *and* look for the ball.

Panthers receiver Mark Carrier is off to the races.

Winning coach
Dom Capers led the Panthers for their first four NFL seasons.

Early in the final quarter, San Francisco's Derek Loville scored on a 6-yard run. The score helped the 49ers avoid their first shutout in 18 years (a shutout occurs when one team does not score in a game).

But that score wasn't enough. The Panthers' defense held on for the final 10 minutes of the game.

The 49ers' fans and players were stunned as the Panthers celebrated their amazing upset victory.

The expansion Panthers had done something no other first-year team had done: defeated the defending NFL champions.

"I'm still on cloud nine," McKyer said.

"It seemed impossible for a rookie team to come in and win," Panthers quarterback Collins said. "Today it happened."

Carolina went on to finish its first season with seven victories, the most ever by a first-year team.

But the biggest victory of that amazing first season came in San Francisco with the Panthers' big upset over the 49ers.

"That was a very special day for us," Panthers coach Dom Capers said.

Special? It was one of a kind.

The Panthers warm up before another game.

Other new teams
Other recent expansion teams include the Tampa Bay Buccaneers (1976), the Seattle Seahawks (1976), and the Cleveland Browns (1999).

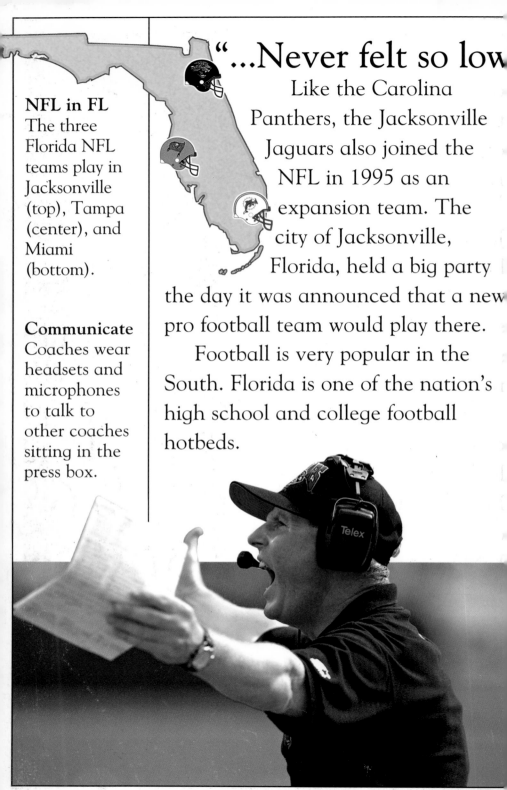

NFL in FL
The three Florida NFL teams play in Jacksonville (top), Tampa (center), and Miami (bottom).

Communicate
Coaches wear headsets and microphones to talk to other coaches sitting in the press box.

Like the Carolina Panthers, the Jacksonville Jaguars also joined the NFL in 1995 as an expansion team. The city of Jacksonville, Florida, held a big party the day it was announced that a new pro football team would play there.

Football is very popular in the South. Florida is one of the nation's high school and college football hotbeds.

The Jaguars joined two other Florida-based NFL teams: the Miami Dolphins and the Tampa Bay Buccaneers.

The fans in Jacksonville expected big things from their new team. But new teams usually start slowly. In their first season, the Jaguars had a record of 4-12.

But they had an exciting young offense led by quarterback Mark Brunell and receivers Keenan McCardell and Jimmy Smith.

Coach Tom Coughlin built the Jaguars from the ground up. He and his staff learned from their tough first season. And in 1996, they were ready to improve.

Southpaw
Left-handed passers such as Jacksonville's Mark Brunell are rare in the NFL.

The Jaguars surprised everyone by finishing their second season with a 9-7 record. It was the second-best record ever by a team in its second season.

Jacksonville earned a "wild-card" spot in the AFC playoffs. Wild-card teams are ones that didn't finish first, but had records good enough to make the playoffs.

Although Jacksonville earned its way into the postseason, few people expected them to go very far.

Buffalo Bills
Playing in Buffalo in upstate New York, the team is named for a famous cowboy, "Buffalo Bill" Cody.

Buffalo's Thomas (34) runs in for one of his two touchdowns.

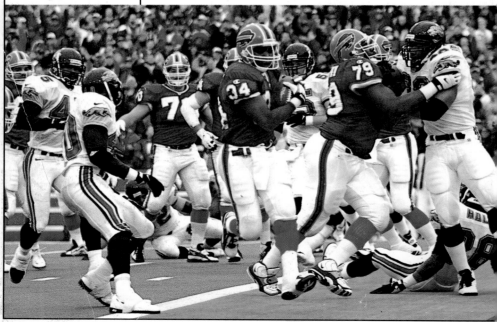

After all, this was a young team, and playoff games are usually won by more experienced teams.

In the first round of the playoffs, the Jaguars traveled to Buffalo, New York, to play the Bills. Buffalo had never lost a playoff game in its home, Rich Stadium (below), which was always filled with rabid fans.

The game started well for Buffalo. Thurman Thomas scored two touchdowns in the first quarter. Jacksonville scored when defensive end Clyde Simmons returned an interception 20 yards for a touchdown.

But Buffalo led 14-10 after one quarter.

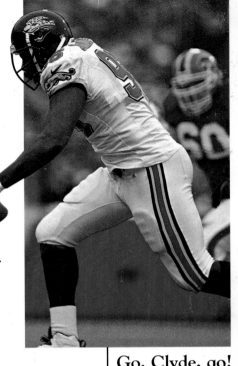

Go, Clyde, go! Jacksonville's Clyde Simmons rumbled 20 yards for a key Jaguars' touchdown.

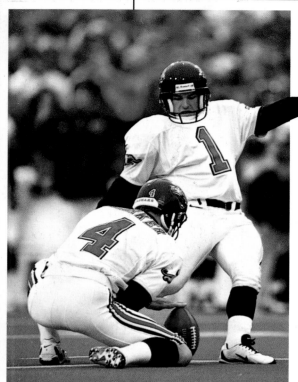

Jaguars running back Natrone Means emerged as a force in the second quarter. He scored on a 30-yard run.

The score was tied 17-17 at halftime.

Buffalo took a 27-20 lead early in the fourth quarter when Jeff Burris returned an interception 38 yards for a touchdown.

But Jacksonville wasn't finished. The Jaguars ignored the screaming of the local Buffalo fans and drove back downfield.

Team effort
A player called the "holder" takes the snap and positions the ball for the kicker to kick.

King Kelly
Jim Kelly (12) led the Bills to four AFC championships from 1990 to 1993.

A key to Jacksonville's success was the play of tackle Tony Boselli. Only a rookie, he held Buffalo's all-pro defensive end Bruce Smith without a sack.

"He did a good job," Smith said.

The Jaguars scored again on a 2-yard pass from Brunell to Jimmy Smith.

That tied the score at 27-27. Then the Jaguars' defense came up with a big play. Chris Hudson forced a fumble by Buffalo quarterback Jim Kelly. The Jaguars had one more chance.

Mike Hollis made a 45-yard field goal for the winning points. The upstarts had shocked the big boys!

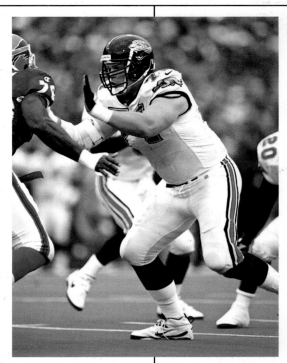

Blocker
Linemen like Boselli stop the defense.

Run wild
Means ran for 175 yards in the game.

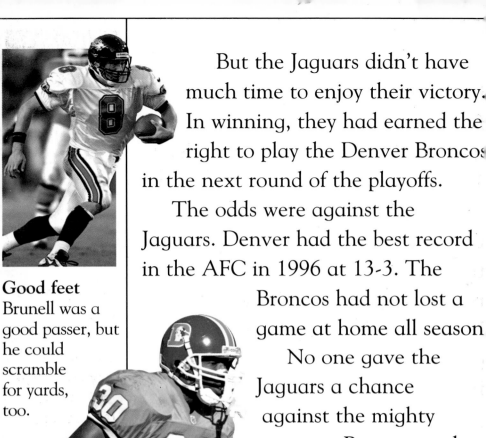

But the Jaguars didn't have much time to enjoy their victory. In winning, they had earned the right to play the Denver Broncos in the next round of the playoffs.

The odds were against the Jaguars. Denver had the best record in the AFC in 1996 at 13-3. The Broncos had not lost a game at home all season. No one gave the Jaguars a chance against the mighty Broncos and their star quarterback, John Elway.

No one except the Jaguars themselves, of course.

Good feet
Brunell was a good passer, but he could scramble for yards, too.

Denver was powered by rookie running back Terrell Davis.

Unfortunately, the Jaguars made it even harder on themselves by falling behind 12-0 after the first quarter. But they came back to lead 13-12 at halftime.

The Jaguars just kept rolling in the second half. They opened the third quarter with a 31-yard touchdown pass from Brunell to McCardell. A field goal by Hollis gave the Jaguars a 23-12 lead early in the fourth quarter.

But the fun was just beginning.

Elway, one of the greatest "comeback" artists in NFL history, led the Broncos down the field. Running back Terrell Davis scored on a 2-yard run, then made a 2-point conversion. The Broncos were within three points.

One of the best Elway combined a powerful arm with great leadership.

This statue of a rearing horse stands atop Denver's Mile High Stadium. A bronco is a type of horse.

Once again, however, the young Jaguars ignored the pressure and drove the ball downfield. Brunell was the key to this important drive.

Twice he scrambled for first downs, once gaining 29 yards.

With just under five minutes remaining in the game, Brunell threw a 16-yard scoring pass to Smith. The score was 30-20, Jacksonville.

A miracle was happening right before the stunned Denver crowd.

The awesome Elway made one last, valiant effort.

He moved his team 80 yards in less than two minutes. He threw a touchdown pass to Ed McCaffrey that brought Denver back to within three points.

But the Jaguars recovered an onside kick and time ran out.

Jacksonville had pulled off one of the biggest upsets in NFL playoff history. The Jaguars stormed the field, high-fiving each other.

Meanwhile, the Denver players were in shock. A season that was supposed to end in the Super Bowl had ended early.

"I have never felt as low as I feel right now," said star Denver tight end Shannon Sharpe. "I can't believe it."

Coach Coughlin had another opinion.

"I told the players I believed they could win," he said. "I am so proud of these guys."

Happy Jaguars linebacker Kevin Hardy was all smiles after the win.

Sad Denver tight end Shannon Sharpe spoke for his teammates.

AFC EAST

Buffalo Bills

Indianapolis Colts

Miami Dolphins

New England Patriots

New York Jets

AFC CENTRAL

Baltimore Ravens

Cincinnati Bengals

Cleveland Browns

Jacksonville Jaguars

Pittsburgh Steelers

Tennessee Titans

AFC WEST

Denver Broncos

Kansas City Chiefs

Oakland Raiders

San Diego Chargers

Seattle Seahawks

AFC teams
These are the 16 teams in the AFC.

Who's next?

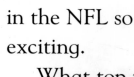

Each week in the NFL, top teams take on teams that are struggling. And often, one of those struggling teams finds a way to win.

Not all the upsets are as big as the ones in this book. But knowing that they can happen "on any given Sunday" is one of the things that makes life in the NFL so exciting.

What top team will be the next to fall to an underdog? When will the Super Bowl champion lose to another last-place team?

Will a championship contender get knocked off by a team with no hope of making the playoffs?

The stories of upsets like these give hope to every team and every player in every game.

Just ask Joe Namath.

Just ask Otto Graham and Paul Brown.

Just ask the Carolina Panthers.

Or just ask Mark Brunell and the Jacksonville Jaguars.

No one expected those teams to win, but they did.

Who's next?

NFC EAST

Arizona Cardinals

Dallas Cowboys

New York Giants

Philadelphia Eagles

Washington Redskins

NFC CENTRAL

Chicago Bears

Detroit Lions

Green Bay Packers

Minnesota Vikings

Tampa Bay Buccaneers

NFC WEST

Atlanta Falcons

Carolina Panthers

New Orleans Saints

St. Louis Rams

San Francisco 49ers

NFC teams
These are the 15 teams in the NFC.

Glossary

Cornerback
A defensive position responsible for covering opposing receivers.

End zone
Ten-yard areas at each end of a football field in which touchdowns are scored.

Field goal
Three-point scoring play in which the football is kicked from the ground over the crossbar and between the uprights of the goalpost.

Fumble
Happens when a player carrying the football drops it on the field of play. Can be recovered by either team.

Interception
Occurs when a defensive player catches a pass intended for an offensive player.

Linebacker
A defensive position that plays behind the defensive line; responsible for stopping runners, covering receivers, and rushing the quarterback.

Quarterback
The key offensive position; calls plays, makes passes and handoffs.

Rookie
A player in his first NFL season.

Roster
A list of the names and numbers of the football team's players.

Sack
When a quarterback is tackled behind the line of scrimmage.

Super Bowl
The NFL's championship game, played each January between the AFC and NFC champions.

Touchback
Occurs when the ball is knocked through the defensive team's end zone or is caught and downed in the end zone by a return team.

Touchdown
Six-point scoring play in which the football is caught in or carried into the end zone.

Underdog
The team not expected to win.

Upset
Occurs when a team not expected to win does win.

Index